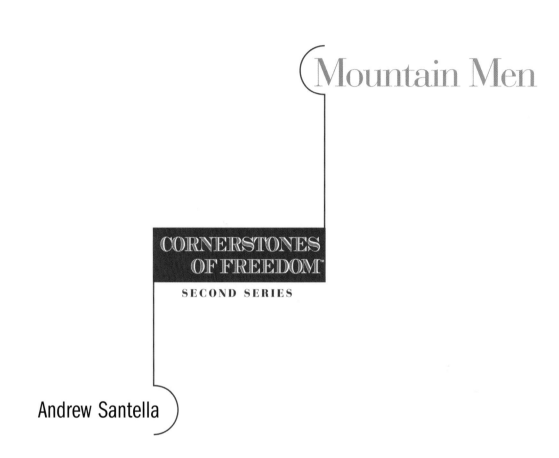

Mountain Men

CORNERSTONES OF FREEDOM™

SECOND SERIES

Andrew Santella

Children's Press®
A Division of Scholastic Inc.
New York • Toronto • London • Auckland • Sydney
Mexico City • New Delhi • Hong Kong
Danbury, Connecticut

Photographs © 2003: Art Resource, NY/Smithsonian American Art Museum, Washington, DC: 14, 17, 24, 28, 34, 37, 40; Corbis Images: 8 (Bettmann), 4 (Burstein Collection), cover top, 39 (Francis G. Mayer); Hulton|Archive/Getty Images: 5, 6, 21, 27, 45 bottom; Joslyn Art Museum, Omaha, Nebraska: 3, 7, 23, 32, 44 bottom; Kansas State Historical Society: 26, 45 top left; Missouri Historical Society, St. Louis/David Schultz: 11; Nativestock.com/Marilynn "Angel" Wynn/Montana Historical Museum: 9, 44 top left; North Wind Picture Archives: 16, 19, 30, 44 top right, 45 top right; Photo Researchers, NY/Tom McHugh: 31, 38; Stock Montage, Inc.: 35 (The Newberry Library), cover bottom, 20; Superstock, Inc./Huntington Library: 12, 13, 41.

Library of Congress Cataloging-in-Publication Data
Santella, Andrew.
  Mountain Men / Andrew Santella.
    p. cm. — (Cornerstones of freedom. Second series)
  Summary: A description of the mountain men, nineteenth-century explorers, and fur traders who helped open up the West to United States settlement.
  Includes bibliographical references and index.
    ISBN 0-516-24216-4
    1. Pioneers—West (U.S.)—History—19th century—Juvenile literature. 2. Explorers—West (U.S.)—History—19th century—Juvenile literature.3. Fur traders—West (U.S.)—History—19th century—Juvenile literature. 4. Trappers—West (U.S.)—History—19th century—Juvenile literature. 5. Frontier and pioneer life—West (U.S.)—Juvenile literature. 6. West (U.S.)—History—To 1848—Juvenile literature. 7. West (U.S.)—Discovery and exploration—Juvenile literature. 8. West (U.S.)—Biography—Juvenile literature. [1. Explorers—West (U.S.)—History—19th century. 2. Fur traders—West (U.S.)—History—19th century. 3. Frontier and pioneer life. 4. West (U.S.)—History—To 1848.] I. Title. II. Series: Cornerstones of freedom. Second series.
F592.S25 2003
978'.02'0922—dc21

                                                    2003005616

1 2 3 4 5 6 7 8 9 10 R 12 11 10 09 08 07 06 05 04 03

ATTENTION! ENTERPRISING *young men needed! The subscriber wishes to engage ONE HUNDRED MEN, to ascend the river Missouri to its source, there to be employed for one, two, or three years. For particulars enquire of Major Andrew Henry, near the Lead Mines, in the County of Washington, (who will ascend with, and command party) or to the subscriber at St. Louis.*

Wm. H. Ashley

So read the advertisement placed by a St. Louis businessman, February 13, 1822, in the Missouri *Gazette & Public Advertiser*, then, in the St. Louis *Enquirer* two weeks later. That spring, hundreds of young men would begin traveling west up the Missouri River. They were headed for the wild Rocky Mountains, in search of adventure and riches.

This Albert Bierstadt painting of California's Yosemite Valley, which few Americans had ever seen, caused a sensation when it was first displayed back in the East.

Most had never seen the Rockies. Many were farm boys from back east, and some were still teenagers. But within a few years, many of these same young men would gain fame as the best of the mountain men.

Mountain men blazed most of the first trails west across the Rocky Mountains in the early 1800s. They were rugged frontiersmen who learned to survive alone in the wilderness. They withstood the bitter cold of the mountain passes and the dangerous heat of the vast deserts. They defended themselves against huge and fearsome grizzly bears. They did battle with American Indian war parties determined to protect their homelands.

* * * *

In the process, the mountain men pointed the way west for the thousands of settlers that followed them. The peak of the mountain man era stretched across the 1820s and 1830s. During that time, mountain men helped draw some of the first maps of the American West. They discovered desert trails and mountain passes wide enough and safe enough for families in covered wagons to one day cross. They brought back the first descriptions of some of the strangest and most wonderful sights of the American West.

What made the mountain men risk their lives in the unexplored West? Many were driven by a thirst for adventure and the urge to go places few people had gone before. But mountain men also knew that there was money to be made in the wild country. The key to wealth was a small animal found in great numbers in the icy streams of the Rocky Mountains. It had a wide, flat tail, huge front teeth—and most important to the mountain men—a thick coat of fur. It was the beaver. Beavers could be found in many parts of

This illustration of a beaver was done in about 1800. Native only to the well-watered woodlands of North America, the beaver was the prize that drove the North American fur trade. Beaver skins were heavily desired in Europe to make top hats; the skins were so valuable in North America that they could be used in many places as a kind of currency or money.

THE ROCKY MOUNTAIN BEAVER

By 1800, hunters and trappers had already begun to kill off great numbers of beavers in the eastern United States and Canada. However, because hunters and trappers were not yet working in the Rocky Mountains, beavers remained plentiful there. Also, Rocky Mountain beavers had especially thick fur to protect them from the icy cold of the mountains. This thick fur made them very desirable to fur traders.

North America, but nowhere was the animal more plentiful than in the western mountains.

Their fur **pelts** were highly prized by the makers of men's hats in Europe and the United States. Every fashionable man in Europe and the big cities of the United States had to own a hat made of beaver. The demand for beaver pelts was so high that a fur trader who gathered enough beaver pelts could make a fortune. But the mountain man's job was full of risks, as well. He might spend a year gathering furs only to lose everything to thieves! A single mistake paddling his canoe down a flooded river and all his furs might sink to the bottom.

This late 18th-century illustration depicts the original American colonists trading furs with an Indian of an eastern tribe. The American fur trade began in the dense woodlands of the original thirteen colonies.

The trappers and hunters who went west in 1822 were part of a growing fur trade. They included some of the most famous names in the history of the mountain men, including Jedediah Smith and Jim Bridger. Mountain men such as these were the first businessmen of the American West. They went west to trap beaver and to trade and sell beaver pelts. In fact, they did their jobs too well. The mountain men were such effective trappers that they nearly wiped out the beaver.

This is the painter Alfred Jacob Miller's portrait of the man he called "Captain Walker," probably the great western trailblazer Joseph Walker. The great mountain men were free spirits, guides, traders, merchants, and explorers. Because the age of the mountain men took place before the development of photography, the work of painters such as Miller, George Catlin, and Karl Bodmer was the way most Americans received a visual introduction to the American West.

Thomas Jefferson was an enthusiastic believer in America's westward expansion. As president, his greatest act in support of that belief was the purchase from France of the Louisiana Territory, more than 800,000 square miles of land between the Mississippi River and the Rocky Mountains.

BEFORE THE MOUNTAIN MEN

Mountain men worked in a land of mystery. In the early 1800s, Americans knew very little about the interior of the American West. A few fur traders and explorers had traveled up the Missouri River, but the mountains, deserts, and plains beyond were still unexplored. When Thomas Jefferson was elected president in 1800, he made up his mind to send an **expedition** to this new frontier. Jefferson wanted to know more about the land west of the Mississippi River and the American Indians who lived on it. He hoped to learn what sorts of plants and animals could be found there. Most of all, he wanted to know if there was a way for people to travel by river across North America. If such a route existed, people and goods could travel quickly across the continent.

Jefferson sent Meriwether Lewis and William Clark to explore the West and to look for a water route to the Pacific. In May 1804, Lewis, Clark, and their 45-person Corps of Discovery began their long journey. They left St. Louis in three boats, heading up the Missouri River. It took them over a year to reach the Pacific Ocean. Blocking their way were some of the tallest mountains they had ever seen. Along the way they had to leave their boats behind and travel long and

A modern artist's rendition of the Lewis and Clark expedition traveling on the Missouri River. Recognizing the money that could be made in the fur trade in the areas the expedition had explored, two of its members, John Colter and George Drouillard, immediately returned to the wilderness.

grueling miles by foot and on horseback. After reaching the Pacific, they finally made it back to St. Louis on September 23, 1806. It was more than two years since they'd left. Most people had given them up for dead.

Lewis and Clark didn't find the easy water passage that Thomas Jefferson hoped for. Instead, they had to march across mountain passes covered in deep snow. But the Lewis and Clark expedition succeeded in teaching Americans a great deal about the unknown West. One bit of news that Lewis and Clark reported was especially interesting to some of the businessmen of St. Louis. The icy streams of the Rocky Mountains were teeming with beaver. A hardworking trapper could easily collect enough beaver pelts to make him rich. News like that traveled very quickly. Even before Lewis and Clark returned to St. Louis, the era of the Rocky Mountain fur trade had begun.

THE FIRST MOUNTAIN MEN

On their way home, Lewis and Clark saw the first wave of the western fur trade up close. They and the Corps of Discovery were making their way back to St. Louis in 1806 when they came upon two men in a canoe on the Missouri River. The men were Joseph Dickson and Forest Hancock, and they were trappers headed for the same wild country that Lewis and Clark had just explored. The members of the Corps of Discovery stopped to tell Dickson and Hancock what they could expect to find up the river. One of Lewis and Clark's men even offered to join Dickson and Hancock. John Colter had just endured more than two years of hardship with Lewis and Clark, but he still wanted to return to the mountains. As a reward for his hard work and reliability, Lewis and Clark let Colter leave the expedition early and go west with Dickson and Hancock.

Colter spent the next three years trapping and exploring in what is now Montana and Wyoming. No one knows what happened to his partners, Dickson and Hancock. Like many mountain men, they ventured into the wilderness and were never heard from again. But Colter became one of the best-known of the mountain men.

In 1807, Colter joined an expedition organized by a St. Louis businessman named Manuel Lisa. Lisa hired about 40 men to travel west to gather beaver pelts. Lisa and his men made their way to what is now Montana, where the Yellowstone and Bighorn rivers meet. There they built a simple log structure called Fort Raymond, in honor of Lisa's son. No white men had ever built a trading post that deep in the wilds of the west. Lisa sent his hired men across the mountains and valleys to spread word to the Indians that he was ready to trade knives, blankets, rifles, and other valuables for furs. Then he waited for the furs to come pouring into Fort Raymond.

This is the only known portrait of Manuel Lisa made from life. Born in Cuba, Lisa is known as Nebraska's first white settler. From his head-quarters in St. Louis, Missouri, Lisa was one of the first merchants to make large profits from the western fur trade.

A STRANGE DISCOVERY

In the winter of 1807–1808, John Colter explored much of what is now Yellowstone Park.

Near present-day Cody, Wyoming, he found a place where fountains of water bubbled and shot

straight out of the earth. Some doubted Colter's stories about the place. However, modern-day

vacationers travel to see the **geysers** of Yellowstone National Park, not far from where

Colter reported his bubbling hot springs.

None of Lisa's men covered more ground or faced more danger than John Colter. His toughness and his ability to survive any peril set the standard for mountain men to follow.

COLTER'S RUN

In 1808, Colter was traveling in western Montana with a trapper named John Potts. The two were surprised and surrounded by Blackfoot warriors. Potts tried to escape and was killed. Colter had no choice but to surrender. He feared he would be killed, too, but the Blackfoot gave Colter one chance to save himself. They took all his belongings, including his clothes, and told him to start running across the **plains**. Colter did as he was told. The Blackfoot warriors first gave

Karl Bodmer (1809–1893) was another of the important artists who traveled the American West and painted it during the era of the mountain men. This is his painting of the Mandan villages on the Missouri River, where Lewis and Clark stayed near the beginning and end of their famous "voyage of discovery."

According to George Catlin, Buffalo Bull's Back Fat, whom he painted in 1832, was a chief of the Blackfoot people. Allied already with British Canadian fur traders, the Blackfoot opposed the mountain men's efforts to expand the American fur trade in the West.

Colter a head start and then began chasing after him. Colter was in a race for his life.

Even running barefoot, Colter was fast enough to leave most of the Blackfoot behind. However, one warrior kept gaining ground on the mountain man. Looking over his shoulder, Colter could see the warrior getting closer and closer. So he stopped in his tracks and turned to fight. The warrior lunged at Colter with his spear, but missed. Seeing his chance, Colter wrestled the spear away and stabbed the warrior with it.

Still, Colter was not out of danger. By now, the rest of the Blackfoot were catching up and determined to kill him. He kept running until he reached the Jefferson River, and there he dove underwater. He hid under floating **driftwood** until the Indians went away. As soon as he could, Colter emerged from his hiding place and began heading for Fort Raymond. Still fearing that the Blackfoot were following, Colter moved as quickly as he could. Finally, naked and starving, he staggered to the gates of the fort. He had covered more than 200 miles in eleven days.

Colter survived his race with the Blackfoot, and he survived several more brushes with death. Finally, in 1809, he vowed to leave the mountains behind. He returned to Missouri, married, and spent the rest of his days living the quiet life of a farmer.

MOUNTAIN MAN MAPS

While living in Missouri, Colter met with his old commander, William Clark. He told Clark about his travels in the mountains, and Clark used those reports to draw one of the first accurate maps of the central Rocky Mountains. Another member of the Lewis and Clark expedition became a mountain man. He was George Drouillard, and he drew a map of the area around the Yellowstone and Bighorn rivers. It was the first map made by a mountain man.

★ ★ ★ ★

THE LIFE OF THE MOUNTAIN MAN

When a mountain man showed up in St. Louis or another western town, he never failed to turn heads. His very appearance amazed people. After a year or so in the mountains, his face was weather-beaten by exposure to the sun and to the wind. His hair was tangled and long, hanging beyond his shoulders. His clothes were worn-out and filthy. The mountain man might be missing fingers or toes lost to **frostbite**. Or he might carry scars on his body from battles with Indians or encounters with grizzly bears.

A contemporary described the typical clothing of a mountain man as consisting of an antelope-skin shirt, leather pants, a coat made of a blanket or buffalo robe, a hat made of wool or the skin of a buffalo or otter, and moccasins made from the hides of buffalo or elk. Most wore their hair very long and loose, falling down to their shoulders.

16

★ ★ ★ ★

Catlin's *Dying Buffalo Bull in a Snowdrift*. The success of the mountain men did much to bring about the large-scale settlement of the West that would cause the near extinction of the bison and the end of the traditional way of life of the Native Americans.

But it wasn't just the mountain man's wild appearance that impressed towns-people. They respected the mountain man for his ability to survive alone in the wild. Mountain men often worked by themselves or in small teams. Like John Colter, they might find themselves in danger hundreds of miles from their friends and partners. The mountain man had to rely on his own intelligence and toughness to survive. He also had to master a long list of skills. He had to be able to make his own clothes and his own shoes from the skin of deer or buffalo. He had to be able to hunt and fish well enough to feed himself. He had to be smart enough to avoid conflicts with

THE MOUNTAIN MAN DIET

When there was plenty of game to hunt, mountain men might eat up to ten pounds of meat in a day. Buffalo hump and beaver tail were favorites, but horsemeat would do in a pinch. One of the most popular dishes among mountain men was **boudin**, a kind of pudding made from the stomach of bison. However, the mountain man had to be prepared for lean times, as well. He almost always carried pemmican, a dried, chewy meat that was easy to carry on long trips.

17

other people, but tough enough to survive when a battle broke out. Most of all, he was a businessman. He had to see that his beaver skins made it safely to the market and were traded for a fair price. As an early western traveler named Rufus B. Sage put it: "A mountain man is his own manufacturer, tailor, shoemaker and butcher."

TRAPPING BEAVERS

When the first Europeans came to North America, the beaver thrived all over the continent. American Indians had trapped beavers for centuries. They made clothing of beaver fur and ate beaver meat. They used cone-shaped woven baskets to catch the beaver.

Europeans soon came to prize the beaver, as well. They traded with Indians for beaver pelts, then began trapping the beavers themselves. Europeans used steel traps that caught beavers by their legs and held them underwater until they drowned. The trapper would set his traps wherever he saw signs of beaver, such as fallen trees. He would set his traps a few inches below water, which often meant wading into ice-cold mountain streams. Nearby the trapper placed a stick smeared with castoreum, a natural fluid produced by the beaver. The smell of castoreum would attract beavers and they would step into the traps.

The trapper skinned the beavers he caught and scraped all the fat and flesh away from the pelt. Then, back at camp, he would stretch the pelt out to dry on a hoop made of willow **saplings**. Once dried, each pelt was folded and pressed down into a bundle of about sixty pelts. When they had trapped as many beaver as they could in one area, they would move on to the next area. Their goal was to gather as many beaver pelts as possible and not leave any beavers for competing trappers. This method was all too effective. Using this method, trappers quickly killed off beaver populations in many parts of North America.

ASTOR'S DREAM

The dream of making loads of money in the mountains made the fortune of one of the richest men in the United States. His name was John Jacob Astor. A German immigrant, Astor's New York City company had made a fortune trading furs from Canada. He planned to build a string of trading posts that stretched from the Missouri River to the Pacific Ocean. Astor's traders would collect furs there and send them to markets all around the world. Astor's first trading post was to be at the mouth of the Columbia River in what is now Oregon. It was going to be called Astoria.

However, Astoria was troubled from the very beginning. In 1810, Astor sent a group of workers to begin building Astoria. They took the long and dangerous sea route—from the east coast of the United States, around the southern tip of South America, and back north through the Pacific

The German immigrant John Jacob Astor made a fortune in the fur trade without ever setting a trap himself. Trained as a maker of musical instruments, Astor arrived in New York City at the end of the Revolutionary War with less than $25 and seven flutes. He quickly became one of the country's richest men by establishing a monopoly on the fur trade in the Pacific Northwest and investing the profits in real estate in New York City.

19

This is Astoria, the trading post and colony established in 1810 by John Jacob Astor's Pacific Fur Company on the Columbia River in what is now Oregon. This 19th-century engraving was based on a drawing made in 1813 by Gabriel Franchere, a French-Canadian who was among the founders of Astoria.

Ocean to the Columbia River. Astor's ship made it safely to the Columbia River and his men began building the trading post. Then disaster struck. Astor's ship was attacked by a group of Indians not far from Astoria. They massacred the crew and blew up the ship.

Astor's western fur business suffered another blow when the War of 1812 broke out between the United States and Great Britain. British fur trading companies were already doing business in the area around Astoria. Now in the face of their open hostility, Astoria had little chance of success. In 1813, Astor's partners sold Astoria to the British Northwest Company.

However, Astoria was not a complete failure. The enterprise produced one of the most important discoveries of the mountain man era. In 1812, a group of Astor's traders led by Robert Stuart traveled east from Astoria to St. Louis. They were carrying business reports back to Astor. In what is now Utah, they were attacked by Crow warriors and lost their way. Trying to find food and a way across the mountains, they stumbled upon a wide green meadow of gentle, rolling hills. It was a break in the long chain of mountains that cut across North America. They had found a path across the mountains wide enough and

This photograph of two travelers in the snowy Canadian Rockies was taken well over 100 years after the mountain men first saw magnificent scenes like this one. However, the vista has not changed all that much since that time.

smooth enough even for heavy wagons. The path came to be called South Pass, and some people recognized its importance right away. One newspaper reported that "a journey across the continent of North America might be performed by a wagon." If wagons could cut through the mountains, then families of settlers could one day move west in those wagons. Eventually, South Pass became the doorway to the West. But it would be another twelve years before another expedition traveled through South Pass. And it would be another twenty years before wagon trains rolled through.

"ENTERPRISING YOUNG MEN"

After the failure of John Jacob Astor's western fur operation, ten years passed before another major expedition was launched. Then, in 1822, William Ashley placed his ad, searching for the "enterprising young men."

Besides being a St. Louis businessman, Ashley was also the lieutenant governor of Missouri and brigadier general of the state militia. Now, he had a plan for a new way to strike it rich in the fur trade. Most other fur companies built forts and trading posts in the wild. Then, they worked to convince local Indians to bring their beaver skins to the fort, where they could trade them for hatchets, knives, kettles, and other valuable items. Ashley built no permanent forts and he didn't try to trade with Indian trappers. Instead, he hired his own trappers—the one hundred "enterprising young men" of the newspaper ad—and supplied them with everything they needed to

The man on the white horse in this Alfred Jacob Miller painting is Sir William Drummond Stewart, a wealthy Scottish nobleman who organized a lavish expedition across the West in 1837. Stewart paid Miller to accompany him and document the journey in paintings and drawings.

trap beaver, including traps, horses, and weapons. Their job was to spend autumn, winter, and spring in the mountains gathering beaver pelts. In the summer, they would bring their pelts to Ashley, buy new supplies, and receive their pay for their year's work.

To make his system work, Ashley set up an annual meeting in the mountains. Each summer, his trappers would gather from all directions in a pre-arranged location. The

This is Catlin's portrait of Wild Sage, a Wichita woman. Many Native American women played an important role in the fur trade as guides, interpreters, and wives for the mountain men. Preparing animal hides for trade was also work often performed by Native American women.

purpose of the meeting may have been to sell furs and buy supplies, but it soon turned into the wildest party the mountains had ever seen! After a year working alone in the cold and snowy mountains, the trappers were ready for fun in the summer sunshine. They competed in foot races and wrestling matches and shooting contests. They gambled and fought. They told fantastic stories about their adventures.

Ashley's meeting came to be called the rendezvous. Every summer from 1825 to 1840, mountain men gathered together. The first rendezvous was held on the Green River in what is now southwestern Wyoming. It lasted only a day or two. However, as word spread, the event became bigger and bigger event and included trappers outside of Ashley's company, Indians, and French-Canadians. At the 1826 rendezvous, trappers celebrated the Fourth of July by shooting off their guns and drinking toasts to the United States.

Perhaps Ashley got the most excited about the rendezvous. He made a fortune from them. After the 1826 meeting, he returned to St. Louis with 10,500 pounds of beaver skins. He owed much of his success to the hard work of the "enterprising young men" who answered his newspaper ad. One of them even became Ashley's partner. His name was Jedediah Strong Smith. He probably explored more of the West than any other mountain man.

JEDEDIAH SMITH

Smith was born in 1798 or 1799 in New York state. As a young man, Smith left home looking for a new life in the West. He reached St. Louis in time to answer Ashley's help-wanted ad and join the ranks of the mountain men. He soon learned how dangerous that life could be. In 1823, he was leading a group of trappers through the Black Hills of South Dakota when a grizzly bear attacked. The huge bear first took Smith's head in her mouth, then threw him to the ground. She broke several of Smith's ribs and clawed his face and head, before leaving the mountain man bleeding and badly wounded. His **scalp** and one ear had been nearly torn off his head. Smith's group was hundreds of miles from the nearest doctor, and none of his men knew what to do. Smith took charge. "You must try to stitch me up in some way or other," Smith told his men. A trapper named James Clyman sewed Smith's scalp and ear back on. He bandaged the rest of Smith's wounds and hoped his leader would recover. Incredibly, after ten days of rest, Smith was ready to move on. He bore the scars of the bear attack for the rest of his life.

The following spring, Smith made one of his most important discoveries. He led a group of trappers west in search of a way across the Rocky Mountain ranges of Wyoming. At first they found only snow and cold. Temperatures were so low that the group was afraid to sleep at night for fear of freezing to death. Then they came upon South Pass. This was the same wide mountain meadow

Jedediah Strong Smith made many trips through the American West, but his greatest feat was actually his exploration of the deserts of the American Southwest. Born in upstate New York, Smith was inspired to go west as a teenager by reading the journals of the Lewis and Clark expedition.

Mountain men hunt a grizzly bear in this 1835 illustration. Of all the animals they encountered in the West, mountain men found the grizzly bear the most ferocious and intimidating.

that Robert Stuart and his Astorians had discovered in 1812. Now Smith's men followed the pass into the beautiful valley of the Green River in southwestern Wyoming. They were the first mountain men to travel through the pass since Stuart twelve years earlier.

After Smith's rediscovery of South Pass in 1824, the pass became a highway to the West. First mountain men, then missionaries, then settlers followed Smith through

Catlin's *Prairie Meadows Burning*. Lewis and Clark and other western explorers reported that the Native Americans sometimes intentionally set the plains on fire for celebration or as a way of driving animals in a certain direction.

the pass. South Pass became a key part of the Oregon trail—the route that carried thousands of settlers west to Oregon and California in the 1840s.

Meanwhile, Smith was making a small fortune trapping beaver. In one year, he traded in $5000 worth of furs. With his new wealth, he was able to become part owner of Ashley's fur company. He also kept pushing into unexplored territory. In 1826, he decided to explore the country southwest of the Great Salt Lake in Utah. He led 14 men south through Utah into Arizona. They had trouble finding food and water, and their horses began to die in the heat. Smith's men might have died, too, but they were rescued by Mojave Indians. Eventually, Smith and his men made it to the Spanish mission settlements of San Bernardino in California.

Spanish officials feared that Americans wanted to take over parts of the Spanish territory in the West. They suspected Smith might be a spy. In January 1827, they ordered Smith and his men to return home immediately. Smith headed north through the Central Valley of California, where he found plentiful beaver. By May, he and his men collected 1,500 pounds of beaver pelts. Rendezvous was now just two months off, and Smith looked forward to earning another big profit selling his furs. But first Smith had to find a way back east to the rendezvous. Deep snow made the Sierra Nevada Mountains of California almost impossible to cross. Smith decided to leave some of his men behind with his furs. With a smaller group, he crossed the mountains into modern-day Nevada, just south of Lake Tahoe.

They found themselves back in the desert, again facing terrible heat. During the day, Smith's men buried themselves up to their necks in sand to keep cool. Running out of food, they ate the horses that died on the way. His men were ready to quit, but Smith kept pushing them on. Finally, they reached the Great Salt Lake. Smith wrote that it was "a joyful sight, for we knew we would soon be in a country where we would find game and water."

Smith soon arrived at the rendezvous, to the amazement of the other trappers. He wrote that they "caused considerable **bustle** in camp, for myself and my party had been given up for lost." He had crossed some of North America's

This is a Frederic Remington (1861–1909) portrait of two mountain men. A painter, sculptor, and illustrator, Remington is perhaps the most popular artist of the American West. Although he spent most of his life in the East and lived and worked after the age of the mountain men, Remington's depiction of their clothing and appearance is considered remarkably accurate.

The fierce wolverine was another animal native to North America that the mountain men were among the first whites to encounter. In Native American mythology, the wolverine is often depicted as a trickster and a link to the spirit world; mountain men and trappers, however, referred to the animal as "woods devil" or "Indian devil."

highest mountains and traveled across the largest desert in the United States. In eleven months, he had traveled about 1500 miles. He survived snow, bitter cold, intense heat, and lack of food. Amazingly, after two weeks of rest, he was ready to do it all again.

It was said of Joseph Walker that he did not follow trails, he made them. He was the first white American to cross the Sierra Nevada from east to west and to see the Yosemite Valley.

Smith's furs and some of his men were still stranded in California. In July 1827, he set off for California once more to retrieve them. Again, he traveled south through Utah, into Arizona. However, this time the Mojave were not so friendly. They attacked Smith's group as they tried to cross the Colorado River. Ten of his men were killed. Smith and the rest escaped across the desert, and again made it to the Spanish missions of southern California. Spanish officials were not pleased to see Smith a second time. They took him by ship to San Francisco and again ordered him out of California.

This time, Smith led his men north into Oregon. They were **hampered** by constant rain and attacks by local Indians. In July, Kelawatset warriors struck Smith's camp. Smith and two of his men had ridden ahead to scout. Smith returned to find his men massacred and his furs gone. Smith made it to safety at Fort Vancouver, a British trading post on the Columbia River. He had trapped and explored for two years, and didn't have a single beaver pelt to show for it. Still, Smith's long journeys of 1826 and 1827 stand out among the most remarkable achievements in American history.

In 1830, Smith left the mountains forever. He sold his share of the fur company and returned to Missouri. The next year, he was killed by Comanche warriors along the Santa Fe Trail. He was just thirty-two years old.

WALKER PASS

Mountain man Joe Walker led the first expedition to cross the Sierra Nevada Mountains from Nevada into California. Walker followed a pass that led into the beautiful Yosemite Valley of California. It came to be called Walker Pass, and it was used by thousands of westbound settlers during the 1840s.

LEGENDARY MOUNTAIN MEN

Jim Bridger was one of the most colorful of all the mountain men. Some called Bridger "King of the Mountain Men." Maybe Bridger gave himself that nickname. He was

This is a George Catlin portrait of a Crow woman named *Woman Who Lives in a Bear's Den*. Catlin (1796–1872) was the first American artist to seriously attempt to portray the Native American peoples who populated the West in the age of the mountain men.

A great lover of nature and the wilderness, John James Audubon (1785–1851) is considered America's foremost painter of animal life, especially birds. This is an Audubon portrait of a buffalo (bison), made after his journey in the West of 1843. The mountain men were constantly amazed by the sheer numbers of bison in the West and the size of the herds in which they traveled.

a well-known spinner of boastful "tall tales" about his own adventures. In 1825, Bridger floated down the unexplored Bear River of Utah just to show another trapper that he could do it. Bridger may have been the first white man to see the Great Salt Lake in Utah. When he tasted its salty water, he mistakenly believed he had found an arm of the Pacific Ocean. Later, Bridger founded a trading post named Fort Bridger, on the Oregon Trail. He was one of the last surviving figures of the age of the mountain men. He died in Missouri in 1881.

BRIDGER'S ARMOR

At the 1837 rendezvous, Jim Bridger received an unusual gift from a visiting Scottish nobleman. It was a coat of armor and a **plumed** steel helmet. Bridger proudly paraded up and down in his armor, while his fellow mountain men laughed.

★ ★ ★ ★

Mountain men often had to survive terrible ordeals. The most extreme example might be the story of a trapper named Hugh Glass. Glass was traveling with some other trappers when he was mauled by a grizzly bear in the hills of South Dakota and "tore nearly to peases [pieces]." He had wounds all over his body, and the other trappers were certain he would die. Two trappers stayed behind with the badly wounded Glass, while the others moved on. Soon the two trappers with Glass moved on, too, leaving him for dead. (Some think that Jim Bridger was one of those trappers.) But Glass did not die. He crawled and limped back to Fort Kiowa in modern-day Nebraska. It took him six weeks to cover the 200 miles back to the fort. When he arrived, trappers at the fort didn't even recognize him. "It is Glass before you," he told them. Glass worked as a mountain man for another ten years before he was killed by Arikara warriors in 1833.

Some mountain men traveled all over North America, but one went to Europe, too. His name was Jean-Baptiste Charbonneau. He was the son of Lewis and Clark's only female expedition member, Sacagawea—the Shoshone woman who helped them find horses for their journey across the Rocky Mountains. After Lewis and Clark returned to St. Louis, Clark adopted Jean-Baptiste. He later introduced the boy to a German **nobleman** named Prince Paul of Wurttemburg. The nobleman took the boy back to Germany with him, where he lived among the

Catlin called this painting *Medicine Man, Performing His Mysteries Over a Dying Man.* White fur traders and Native Americans often exchanged information about their cultures' ways of healing.

nobility for six years. However, the life of the mountain man was in Charbonneau's blood. He returned to the mountains, then moved to California, where he died of **pneumonia** in 1866.

THE LAST RENDEZVOUS

The era of the mountain man did not last. By the middle of the 1830s, fashionable men in New York and London were no longer wearing beaver hats. The style had changed to silk top hats. As a result, the demand for beaver pelts

This is Audubon's painting of a Canadian lynx, a member of the cat family that the mountain men encountered in the northern forests of North America.

A contemporary illustration of Fort Laramie, which was founded in southeast Wyoming in 1834 as a trading post. In the late 1840s, the fort became a rest and supply station for the dozens of wagon trains that made their way west each year along the California and Oregon trails.

dropped. For mountain men, it became harder and harder to make a living trapping beaver. More and more of them left the mountains to find new lines of work.

In their wake came settlers and missionaries pushing west. Between 1841 and the start of the Civil War, a "Great Migration" of thousands of settlers moved to California and Oregon. They followed trails blazed by mountain men. In fact, many of them were guided by former mountain men.

Fast Dancer was the name of this Ojibwa warrior painted by Catlin in 1834. Many Indian peoples were successful participants in the fur trade, which enabled them to obtain such things as guns, ammunition, horses, metal goods, woven clothing, and, more destructively, alcohol.

For example, a trapper named Tom Fitzpatrick led the first great wagon train to California in 1841.

The last rendezvous was held in 1840 on the banks of the Green River. It was an unusually quiet gathering. The age of the mountain man was coming to an end. A trapper named Robert Newell summed it up: "We are done . . . with wading in beaver dams, and freezing or starving. . . . The fur trade is dead."

In some ways, mountain men left the West a poorer place. Their trapping ended up killing beaver populations in many parts of the country. To succeed in the fur trade, they made use of land that American Indians thought of as theirs. However, mountain men also helped open the West for the settlers that followed. Their trails led countless settlers to new and better lives in the open spaces of the West.

Catlin painted this picture of Native Americans playing a ballgame something like lacrosse. Although their work helped speed the destruction of traditional Native American culture, the success of a mountain man in his line of work often depended on his ability to forge largely peaceful, productive relationships with the Indians.

Glossary

boudin—a kind of pudding made from the stomachs of bison

bustle—excitement

driftwood—stray pieces of wood floating on water

expedition—a journey organized and made for some specific purpose

frostbite—a dangerous skin condition caused by exposure to extreme cold

geyser—a hot spring that shoots streams of water and steam into the air

hampered—held back or delayed

mission—a church set up in a foreign land to offer religious instruction

nobleman—a person belonging to the wealthiest and most powerful class of a society

pelts—the skins of animals

plains—flat stretches of land

plumed—decorated with a bird's feather or plume

pneumonia—a disorder of the lungs

saplings—young trees

scalp—the skin of the top of the head

Timeline: Mountain

St. Louis businessman Manuel Lisa organizes the first large American fur-trapping expedition.

John Colter traps beaver and explores in what is now Yellowstone National Park.

John Jacob Astor founds Astoria in Oregon.

Robert Stuart leads a group from Astoria across South Pass.

William Ashley organizes his famous fur trapping company and signs on Jedediah Smith.

Lewis and Clark explore from St. Louis to the Pacific Ocean and back.

Men

Smith rediscovers South Pass.

First rendezvous is held on Green River in Wyoming.

Smith begins his two-year exploration through the southwest, reaching southern California.

Last rendezvous is held along the Green River.

45

To Find Out More

BOOKS AND VIDEOS

Allen, John Logan. *Jedediah Smith and the Mountain Men of the American West*. Chelsea House, 1991.

Collins, James L. *The Mountain Men*. Franklin Watts, 1996.

Sundling, Charles W. *Mountain Men of the Frontier*. Abdo and Daughters, 2000.

ONLINE SITES

The Fur Trade
www.endoftheoregontrail.org/road2oregon/sa03furs.html

The Oregon Trail
www.isu.edu/~trinmich/Discovers.html

ORGANIZATIONS

Museum of the Mountain Man
Box 909
Pinedale, Wyoming 82941

www.pinedaleonline.com/mmmuseum

(307) 367-4101

Index

About the Author

Andrew Santella writes for magazines and newspapers, including *Gentlemen's Quarterly* and the *New York Times Book Review*. He is the author of several Children's Press books, including *Daniel Boone and the Cumberland Gap*, *The First Thanksgiving*, *U.S. Presidential Inaugurations*, and *September 11, 2001* for Cornerstones of Freedom, Second Series.